D0857594

AFRICAN
STYLE

•

EDITORIAL DIRECTION
Suzanne Tise-Isoré and Nathalie Bailleux

ART DIRECTION
Valérie Gautier - Studio Flammarion

TRANSLATION
Bernard Wooding

COPY-EDITING
Christine Schultz-Touge

•

DESIGN
Caroline Chambeau - Studio Flammarion

PRODUCTION
Claude Blumental

•

Printed and bound by Garzanti, Italy
© Flammarion Paris 2000
ISBN: 2-08013-681-X
Numéro d'édition: FA 3681
Dépôt légal: April 2000

•

AFRICAN
STYLE

STÉPHANE GUIBOURGÉ

PHOTOGRAPHY BY FRÉDÉRIC MORELLEC

CAPTIONS AND DESIGN BY ANNIE DESGRIPPES

Flammarion

the roots of modernity

"BEAUTY IS THE SPLENDOR OF TRUTH" PLATO

Africa does not exist. Just as some people maintain that love does not exist, only proofs of love, perhaps there are only stories about Africa, tales and legends spread by the *griots*, the marabouts, and a handful of travelers and writers, like shadows on the prairie.

Even if, most often, we refuse to look at the African continent, Africa goes on talking to us and continues to sing about itself. And although it can now be found in our living rooms, on the white walls of our apartments—like a form of unspoken iconoclasm—it remains, even if rediscovered, "condemned" to the realm of decoration, that territory where art, the functional, and the sacred mingle. Africa, that burning land which we will never know fully, brings us back to the essential and makes us aware, in our guarded tranquillity, of what we have lost and what is missing from our lives.

Because Africa does not cheat, we cannot cheat it. Because it has revealed so many men, women, talents, and different aspects of human nature —that part of wild nature, primitive but never barbaric, that each of us carries within ourselves, the wild beast that some nights, we hear so close to our hearts, tugging on its chain—it cannot be deflected from its course for long. "Going to Africa," wrote Michel Leiris, "I hoped finally to awaken my emotions! I'm over thirty, I'm growing old… Will I ever be fresh again?"

Africa is a long river, sometimes dry, but always rushing through the plains, hills, deserts, and mountains, of which the snowy peaks stand out in the distance against a trembling sky. It is children singing and the crazy rhythm of funerals, the tempo of rites of passage, the cry of wild animals and the gaze of women whose silhouettes, painted by their *boubous* and *kangas*, stand out gracefully on the line of the horizon. Africa is the pounding of the pestle on the millet or the sorghum in pots made of earthenware or bark. It is giraffes running at nightfall, their nonchalant croups seeming to rest on a cloud, and the bodies of the Masai that were once abandoned in the middle of the bush. It is that long scar in the center of the earth, the valley where we were born. It is the womb, the first blade that separated us from the world, the Rift.

In each of its landscapes, in each of its movements, at the heart of the slightest melody —the wind in the leaves, dust beating against mats, the flapping canvas of nomads' tents— Africa continues to talk to us, to tell us its stories. Everything we need to clear our eyes of today's visual pollution is at hand: a long wooden bench carved quickly out of bark, a mat thrown on the ground, a bowl fashioned from hide, a club slipped into the belt of a young moran (as in the superb *Hidden Art of the Masai* described by Peter Beard, photographer and friend of Karen Blixen). These objects designed for repose,

combat, or the quenching of thirst become, in their darkness, in their brilliant construction, more than a desire, a need. Something obvious. A primal pleasure.

"Primal" rather than "ethnic," a term that was overused for certain art and artifacts during the 1980s, or "*art nègre*" too closely associated with a trend, spearheaded by the world of jazz and Josephine Baker, which brought African art into Parisian salons and galleries in the 1920s.

Primal in the sense intended by Jean Dubuffet, when he coined the term Art Brut at the end of World War II, characterizing such art as "productions of all kinds—drawings, paintings, embroideries, modeled or sculpted figures—presenting a spontaneous and highly inventive character, as little as possible indebted to usual art or cultural clichés." Primal in the sense of getting back to essentials, going back to the source. Yet also "African" because the bowls, wall hangings, mats, masks, tables, and toys presented in this book—whether authentic or reinterpreted by Western designers—are all inspired by, if not impregnated with, the vast African spaces, and all bear that same stamp.

They are African because they call for the rhythms of that continent. They are African because they come out of African nature. In fact, it is nature that formed the raw materials which people can then work from, carving objects as the days, celebrations, and events dictate.

This book focuses less on materials, colors, patterns, and forms than on elements that we can adapt to, or rather, that we can live with—rain, wind, sun and warmth, sweltering heat, plains or forests, harvests and monsoons, celebrations, endless discussions. These are objects for life itself, at a time when, still suffering from *fin de siècle* exhaustion, sickened by overconsumption, we seem to be seeking our way. It is a time when many of us seem to be struck by an inability to express our pain and our grief, as well as our dreams. It is a time when our mythologies are fading, when our beliefs are searching. Following the example set by many on the French creative scene—from Françoise Hughier to Raymond Depardon, from Xuly-Bët to Jean-Paul Gaultier, from Christian Liaigre to Jérôme Abel Seguin and Marion Lesage, not to mention the kids from the housing projects, the *tchatcheurs*, the rappers who would rather return to their African origins than the facile American model—it is time for us to give ourselves up to the natural, the instinctive, the essential force of African style. We should make Léopold Senghor's words our own:

Ah! to sleep once again
in the cool bed of my childhood
Ah! to have my sleep tucked in once again
by those beloved black hands
and white smile of my mother.
Tomorrow, I'll set off once again for Europe,
set off for the embassy
longing for the black country.

materials

work by Marion Lesage

AFRICAN STYLE, ABOVE ALL, HAS TO DO WITH MATERIALS AND NATURE. NONE OF THE MATERIALS USED HERE HAVE BEEN "CORRUPTED," GENETICALLY MODIFIED OR ARTIFICIALLY REPRODUCED. THEY COME FROM THE EARTH, EMERGING FROM THE DAWN OF TIME, ONLY GRADUALLY SHAPED BY TECHNIQUES ACQUIRED AS HUMANS EVOLVED. NOW, CONTEMPORARY DESIGNERS AND ARCHITECTS ARE REDISCOVERING THESE MATERIALS AND ADAPTING THEM TO CURRENT TASTES.

SISAL, LEATHER, STONE, WOOD, ROOTS, CLAY, TREE TRUNKS, IVORY, STONEWARE, TERRA COTTA—THERE ARE MANY MATERIALS, BUT JUST ONE RULE: AUTHENTICITY.

NOT ONLY DID NATURE PROVIDE THE RAW MATERIALS, IT ALSO, ABOVE ALL, PROVIDED THE INSPIRATION FOR THE FORMS OF THE OBJECTS—THE LINE OF A BENCH, THE CURVE OF A JAR. FINALLY, IT IS HUMAN CULTURE, WITH ITS BELIEFS AND RITES, WHICH HAS SCULPTED, SCARIFIED, AND ADDED A NOTE OF ART BRUT IN COMPLETE HARMONY WITH THE TRADITIONS AND FAITHS OF THE PEOPLE CONCERNED.

IT IS IN THE SIMPLE BEAUTY OF THESE SOMETIMES SLIGHTLY CRUDE OBJECTS, TAKEN FROM THE EARTH, THAT THEIR ORGANIC ESSENCE LIES. THEY ARE BEAUTIFUL BECAUSE THEY SERVE A PURPOSE. THEY HAVE A FUNCTION AND IT WAS UPON THIS ANCESTRAL FUNCTION THAT THE LIVES OF MEN, WOMEN, CHILDREN— AS WELL AS THEIR HERDS OF ANIMALS—DEPENDED. EACH EVERYDAY OBJECT GENERALLY BEARS A DECORATIVE MOTIF INTENDED AS EMBELLISHMENT, BUT WHICH ALSO HAS A MEANING, SUCH AS OWNERSHIP OR ITS SPECIFIC FUNCTION IN EVERYDAY LIFE. FOR US, IN OUR CHOICE OF DECORATION, AFRICA AND ITS ORIGINAL MATERIALS CAN GIVE MEANING IN PLACES WHERE WE NO LONGER KNOW HOW TO CREATE IT.

Everything started, of course, with drawing. Look back to the rock paintings and engravings of the Sahara, where representations of masked dancers from prehistoric civilizations have been discovered. A bit later came the cave paintings of East Africa made with pencils cut direct from a branch. Today, the Manding from West Africa and above all the Bochiman from southern Africa still practice this form of rock art.

mallet and gouge

Detail of scarification made with the tip of a knife on ocher and charcoal stoneware (facing page, top left). Borana pot made of woven rope, used for storing water or milk (facing page, top right).
Detail of the center of a cup in burnt oak, worked with a gouge and mallet (facing page, bottom).
Bench made from oak carved with a gouge, a tool which makes it possible to cut into untreated wood and which is used by African sculptors to execute details and finishing touches. This ancient technique, inherited from African woodworkers, and rediscovered in the 1930s by Jean-Michel Franck, is now inspiring many contemporary designers. The sturdy legs of this bench created by Olivier Gagnère are reminiscent of those found on benches made by the Senufo of the Ivory Coast (right).

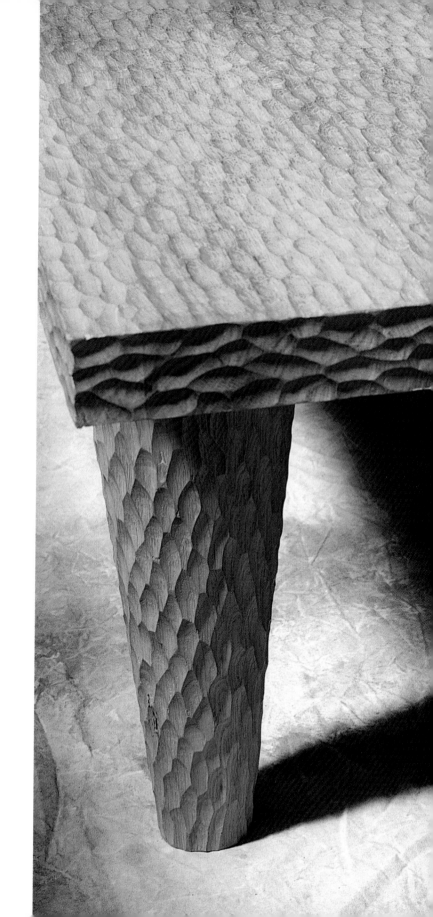

From stone to sand to earth… From the hesitant line drawn by a child in the ocher dust of a village scorched by heat—whether inventing other universes, other horizons between the huts, or simply drawing the faces of those in charge of education, and future initiation—we reach the creations of Marion Lesage on parchment paper. From multicolor frescoes reproduced on the mud or sheet-metal walls of stalls marking the African continent, their sides and roofs rusted by showers and monsoon, to wall lamps and folding screens equally rusted and aged, time does its work in Africa, leaving a patina on each and every object. In the West many designers achieve the same result by oxidizing the metal. Time creates materials, and materials endure the whims of time.

It all begins with water. Water has to be found, carried, and kept. Water, which sometimes lacks and often sanctifies. It is a long walk from the river or well to the village. So bowls and pots are woven of sisal—a fiber from the agave plant, found only south of the equator. Weaving is all that is required, for the rope expands in contact with water, making the vessel watertight. For example, the pretty Borana pots from northern Kenya (see p. 14).

Leather, metal or stone ? In fact, it is made from earth. The piece was created by means of the coil technique, which gives great freedom of form and volume, and it was scarified with a knife tip.

While spinning is a woman's activity, weaving is carried out by men. They use mostly cotton, raffia, or fibers. Picture the women in their long tunics on the banks of the Ruaha River in northwest Tanzania, their nonchalant, swaying silhouettes at nightfall, a cluster of children at their feet sticking their laughing faces under the smallest drop of water which a bump in the ground causes to spill out of the pots that their mothers are balancing on their heads—a way of carrying the head that can only be that of queens.

Helmet mask in dark wood made by the Igala tribe in Nigeria (above). Terra-cotta dish made up of sheets of clay, grooved and then coated in slip. After firing, the oxides in the metal have restored the material's original color (right).

It is not surprising to see how, in their designs of ethnic inspiration, contemporary designers find in African arts and crafts an opportunity to rediscover, to adopt, to be initiated (the choice of term is deliberate) into forgotten techniques, and to consider different supports for their work.

This is the case for the superb drawings by Marion Lesage at the opening of each chapter in this book. Lesage was once a fashion designer for Jacques Estérel, then had her own label before devoting herself to painting. Her oils and watercolors display a profound respect for different cultures and customs. Using supports which are simultaneously old and original, somewhere

Hand carved Indonesian spoons made from palm
and coconut trees; the largest is made
with the gourd of a coconut (top).
Mirror made from chestnut, tinted and scratched
with a gouge (left).

This monumental stoneware pot, raised by means of the coil technique, was colored with ocher and scarified with a knife tip.

Detail of a hewn section of still-green oak (above). Mask made from wood and pigment from Gabon (below).
A contemporary creation based on ancestral know-how: two English designers, sculptor Malcom Martin and textile designer Gaynor Dowling, have combined their talents to produce these monumental "totem sculptures." They are made from oak worked first with a small ax and then with a mallet and gouge (facing page).

between shade and light—basic materials, planks of wood, old manuscripts, parchments salvaged from markets and souks—Marion Lesage tells tales of Africa, in an almost monochrome way, but always set off, as with a spice, by a sudden burst of color, a touch of red, of stronger blue. These stories or playlets, as well as plunging us into an exotic new world, also tell us something about ourselves. Maghreb and Occident both mean the same thing, both point to the West.

Set against a background of rusted metal screens, these large jars from Indonesia, made from palm wood and teak, were carved directly out of solid tree trunks. This highly decorative composition requires a large space (facing page).

marks

# of time

The patina of time has given this metal lance a beautiful rusty appearance so popular with contemporary designers. This object was used as barter currency in Zaire, hence its name of "money" lance (detail, above). A small Senegalese gourd which is perfect hung in a kitchen or simply placed on a pedestal (left).

This stool with square edges is almost primitive. Made from untreated oak, it was carved from the solid tree trunk (facing page).
A work by Jean-Michel Letellier reminiscent of tree bark (above).
Despite its simplicity, this monumental teak tryptich from the island of Sumbawa creates a feeling of immense power (below).

flush with the wood

Natural elements which seem to have been carved by man: an arrangement of roots cut like wooden flowers (above)
and the strange ballet of Indonesian creepers (facing page). Both creations are by Jérôme Abel Seguin.

The beauty of Marion Lesage's modest works
(meaning without effects) rests on little, on
essentials again: it is as if she paints the way she
lives, the way she travels. A nomad who knows
how to put down roots?

The same is true of the creations of Marianne H.
Buus, Malcom Martin, Gaynor Dowling, and
George Peterson. The first uses glass and the
others work in wood. You seem to hear and

see in their work the birth of material, of all materials: earth, wind, and water—the elements. It is as if the elements themselves and not the artists have fashioned these objects. What a supreme quality, that ability to disappear within a work. They take you back so surely to pure and primal nature, that in the detail of a hewn section of holm oak, (see p. 20) in a form that is both vague and yet terribly clear, you can almost see, almost feel, the skin of a pachyderm. A living material.

Originally, Africans also worked stone, ivory, clay, and metals. Ivory was used especially to make jewelry (bracelets, pendants), household items (boxes, goblets), and on occasion small statues. It is a noble material, difficult to carve but highly prized, particularly pieces from the kingdom of Benin, which are by far the most beautiful.
Pottery is the prerogative of women. In West Africa, the potter is the blacksmith's wife. There are no potter's wheels in Africa. Instead, either a mold is used or the clay is built up in rings. Firing takes place over an open fire, of course.
Traditionally, metals were used in feudal kingdoms. In the regions of the Baoule and Ashanti, gold was used to make the chief's decorations (solid gold necklaces, bracelets, etc.) and certain items of furniture which were decorated with thin sheets of gold fixed to the wood. In the case of iron, such groups as the Dogon (Mali) and the Senufo (Ivory Coast) forged it for religious or aesthetic ends.

The top part of a mask of African inspiration displaying beautiful braiding.
It rests on a surface of cut hemp (right).

hemp

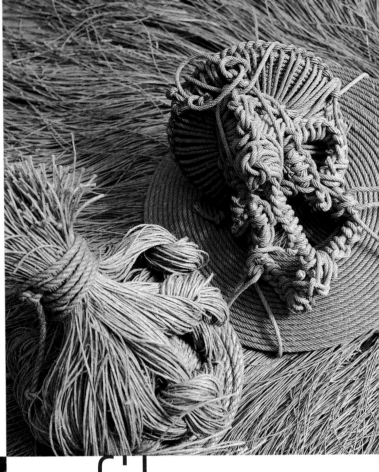

fibers

These little chairs created by Christian Astuguevieille
bring a touch of humor and poetry to an interior.
Both are made from chestnut with the bark intact.
One has a tufted and tousled hemp seat, and the other has a seat
made out of hemp rope and a back in the shape of a child's hut
(facing page and detail left).

But it is wood that recurs most often. It is used everywhere, from Sudan to East Africa, to make statues, masks, and numerous everyday objects such as seats, doors, locks, and containers. The types vary according to the object: soft, light woods for masks, which are thus less heavy to wear, harder woods with a finer grain for furniture.

We always have the impression that these

Placed on a rusted metal garden chair, this poetic lamp consists of a base made from a ball of concrete, a simple branch of chestnut, and a hand-made shade (facing page). Like eggs in a nest, these round soaps made of honey and shea occupy a receptacle made from half a gourd (below).

nature in the raw

various objects have been given to us, delivered to us, with the aim of helping us to live better.

One thinks of Michel Leiris: "Work in Bla with the blacksmiths. Vast group of forges forming a communal workshop. On one wall, a nailed vulture. At Kemeni, located a magnificent Kono cabinet . . . with its compartments filled with skulls and bones of sacrificed animals."

In Mali, Guinea, the Ivory Coast, and the Congo, the wood carver is simultaneously the blacksmith. He is an important figure because he is the possessor of the science of fire-making. In Dogon and Bambara myths, the blacksmith is a civilizing hero, the provider of the primordial techniques of life.

Felt, simple and natural, this sturdy material is being used increasingly in decoration. A shopping bag, light and practical, here becomes an original flower-pot holder (left).

felt

basic

This squat and strikingly simple piece of furniture has two compartments (facing page), while this square, comfortable armchair is adorned with visible topstitching (detail right).

When it comes to the working of iron or wood for a utilitarian and functional or sacred purpose, nothing has really changed. The wood carver starts off with a block that is cylindrical in shape and, without using a model or adding anything to it, he sketches using a machete, through repeated approximate touches. The object itself is formed by means of an adz, and then a short knife, before being polished.

the beauty of stone

Genuine beach stones engraved and transformed into paperweights (left). Fake paving blocks, but real candles (facing page).

The oak bench by Olivier Gagnère (see p. 15) was made in this way. The marks in the wood come from a tool used by African craftsmen and that Jean-Michel Franck rediscovered in the mid-1930s: the gouge. The relationship between the Senufo carvers from the Ivory Coast—who seem to have inspired this extraordinarily pure object—and this established French designer, is more than a filiation, it represents two different paths which come together. In the material itself feelings, beliefs, and sincerity are inscribed.

simply concrete

Concrete is now a full-fledged decorative material. As a replacement for carpets and parquet flooring, it can be left in its raw state (facing page), smoothed, waxed, or even tinted. Numerous objects made out of concrete feature in the collections of contemporary designers, such as this clean-lined cross, which can be used as an ashtray or to hold small change (above).

These objects, some modern, some from collections of African art, go beyond the frontiers of representation. Today, if you hang a sacred mask on the wall, it is in good taste to know where it comes from and what it means, to be able to explain why the material it is carved from is important. That is how a decor is given meaning. Never forget that materials do not lie.

Like wood, metal becomes increasingly beautiful as it ages. Imported from India, these round and square folding stands can be used as occasional or end tables (facing page). Also from India, these dishes, which are traditionally used to make *chapati*, serve perfectly as plates or trays (below).

metal impact

Lightly aged and worked by contemporary designers,
the zinc used on Parisian roofs has been made into original frames (facing page).
Details of sheets of zinc (right and below).

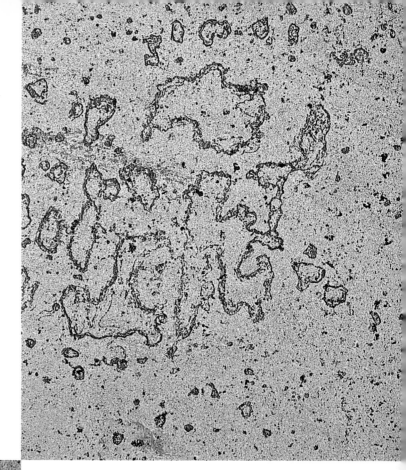

Never forget that African crafts and art, and even the "ethnic fashion" that they have given rise to speak to something buried deep within us. And don't forget, that when a sculpture performs a magical or sacred function, that each mask, each ancestral effigy, conceals a fear, a presence glimpsed at night, a worry or even a terror—that of dying or being alive—and also perhaps a few divinities burning deep within us… Hanging a mask on your wall is never innocuous; it is a fairly significant impulse, it is never the stuff—or material—of chance.

It is as if when finally, after having searched for a long time, dreamt of it for a long time, desired it for a long time, you find in a face the exact definition of love. And the whole world, and the cosmos, are held in this face, like those tribes

who become their art, who mark their skin so that they resemble more closely their ideal, so that they can better rise up toward their divinities. A long way from the man-object, this is the affirmation of the "raw material" man. Is it not said by certain ethnic groups in West Africa when addressing God (or the gods) that "all men came out of your wooden stomach"?

"Our decision is taken quickly: Griaule takes two flutes and slips them into his boots. We put things back where they were and we go out," writes Michel Leiris. These objects—originally pillaged, the bitter fruits of colonization—these works of art and craft, the raw materials, the masks and everyday objects (items of Indonesian cutlery, pieces of grooved pottery from the Congo) which now adorn our homes have exacted a kind of revenge. Now, they also inhabit us. To begin with, perhaps we thought it was a game. Maybe it was a kind of playful innocence, a consumerism looking for new targets, who knows? But there is something else, which we did not know. We thought we were merely combining the ethnic and the aesthetic. Yet the beads we play with once served as currency exchanged for ivory, gold, stones, and slaves. These beads were used by the indigenous people to make adornments, jewelry, quivers, and loincloths. Today they appear on the fashion

Coffee table. The top is covered with a sheet of zinc, simply decorated with nails. The two robust legs are carved out of wood (facing page).
This lamp, with its curved body, represents a marriage of two materials: beech wood and copper (right).

These measuring cups from India have been given a new function.
Turned upside down and fitted with a spike of oxidized metal,
they have been transformed into candle-holders (below).
These enormous Indonesian teak bowls
appear tiny in front of the gigantic screens made of rusted metal.
The shields, standing more than three meters high, were made by a contemporary French designer. The bowls have perforations
that were used to fix drum skins (facing page).

catwalks, "reinvented" by Tom Ford for Gucci, Franck Sorbier, or Jean-Paul Gaultier.

Some tribal societies feel the need, for example, to decorate and paint new initiates. The face, in preparation for make-up, first has to be remodeled, a process which includes removal of hair and scarification. Gradually, the face becomes a veritable mask. This need to model the body can be seen today in tattooing and piercing—African forms of scarification being appropriated by a new generation in the West. It is as if we, such materialistic people, have learned not to be afraid of raw materials. Perhaps a real need for purity and redemption has taken hold of us. Hence we are ready to turn toward our own raw materials. Having measured ourselves through others—their outlook, their art, their ways and materials, we seem capable, now, of speaking about ourselves. We are ready to reveal our everyday selves, sometimes crude, but pared down, essential. Having learned the lesson of African art and craft, we are dispassionate, almost dispossessed. False paving blocks, real stones, zinc and concrete: these materials for so long devoid of meaning, which accompany our everyday lives without us ever seeing anything in them except their utilitarian function, needed nothing other than to be visualized with a new eye, seen by means of the "distant view" so dear to Claude Lévi-Strauss.

Confronted with, or rather laid on top of their alter egos from the Dark Continent, forged anew, reworked, these materials can acquire their real amplitude, their full value, without revolt, but with exactitude. They have become objects, simple decoration. Essential.

Made up of squares of crystallized glass, this coffee table rests on a light metallic structure. The benches, made of patinated zinc, seem to be covered in a shimmering fabric (facing page). This dish made of *pâte-de-verre* and blown glass, the work of Marianne H. Buus, seems to have been sculpted. In fact, the coil technique was used, which consists in winding a thick ribbon of glass, in the form of a hot liquid, which hardens as it cools (below).

opalescent glass

colors

1839 9bre   17   ...me Lalet
1848 aout   9   ...t Perier

Mazeau ...me de la C...
1846 janvier 18   Lagarde
d. février   8   ...rier

Maslie... St Jean de
1848 avril   la Tervenerie

Mastieu pierre

work by Marion Lesage

WHERE ELSE WOULD THE COLORS OF AFRICAN STYLE COME FROM BUT NATURE?

THE MATERIALS THEMSELVES BECOME COLOR, THEN SHADE, THEN DYE: A GIRAFFE IN THE BUSH, ITS SHIMMERING COAT OF YELLOW AND BROWN PATCHES FORMING A SOFT MONOCHROME; THE AROMATIC MARULA BARK STRIPPED BY AN ELEPHANT, REVEALING AN ALMOST FIERY RED; THE CRIES OF THE BIRDS; THE SOARING EAGLES WITH THEIR RED BREASTS, LEAVING AN AIR OF MYSTERY FLOATING OVER THE BLUISH EXPANSE. THEN THERE IS THE OCHER OF THE TRACKS, THE RED OF THE LATERITE PATHS, THE DULL SHADES OF THE CLAY AFTER THE RAIN, THE MIXTURES OF PINK AND MAUVE IN THE HILLS OF KAROO, IN CAPE PROVINCE, SOUTH AFRICA. THE WAY ALL COLORS ARE SOFTENED, POLISHED BY THE SUN AND THE MONSOONS. A LAYER OF COARSE WOOL, A PRAYER RUG, A NOMAD'S CARPET; THE PURPLE OF A YOUNG MASAI'S TOGA, THE COLOR OF KINGS; KINONDONI MARKET, WHERE THE SHADOWS LENGTHEN AS NIGHT FALLS, UNDER THE BIG GRASS HUT, THE BARE FEET IN THE PATHS OF BLACK EARTH; THE BOLD GREEN OF THE WATERMELON RIND AND IT'S RED FLESH; THE LIGHTER GREEN MELONS WITH THEIR PALE ORANGE HEARTS; GREEN BANANAS, ALMOST FUORESCENT IN THE HALFLIGHT; A MANGO, HOT PEPPERS, CLOVES, SPICE—LIKE THE FABRICS ONCE BROUGHT FROM INDIA VIA ZANZIBAR.

THE LAST OF THE SUN'S RAYS CLING TO THE WOMEN'S *BOUBOUS* AND *KANGAS*; A BREEZE CAUSES THE FABRIC TO FLUTTER AND STIRS UP AN OCHER DUST AROUND THEM; FLAME TREES SWAY SLOWLY. RED FLOWERS ARE SUSPENDED IN THE AIR... ALL THE SCENES OF LIFE IN AFRICA ARE LINKED TO AROMAS AND COLORS. THIS IS THE ONLY LAND IN THE WORLD WHERE COLORS HAVE A SMELL—THAT OF PURE SENSUALITY.

Africa is a continent of colors—from the Ndebele of South Africa, whose houses are painted like tropical Mondrians, to the 'Mama Benz' of Ghana, so named because the fabric trade of their famous *batiks* made them rich enough to buy the Mercedez-Benz in which they parade through the streets of Accra.

African artisans used the various warm shades of ocher in the weaving these cushion covers, creating a gentle and natural harmony (facing page). Yellows, browns, and reds—ochers are the basic pigments of African style (below).

born of the earth

This medley of over-sized gourds from Kenya
creates a harmonious composition of reds. The engraved animal friezes
help bring out the color, which is obtained with the help of
a brew of Frugane millet stems (below).
The natural colors of soapstone, which can be found in the Kisli region of Kenya,
range from a milky white and veined pink to yellow and violet.
It can also be dyed and engraved with original designs, as here for
these plates and red dishes with "giraffe" patterns (facing page).

Examples abound and multiply: from the strong colors worn by the Moran (the junior Masai warriors) to the particular weaving techniques of the tribes on the banks of the Kasai River and the Igbo in Nigeria, not forgetting the gold jewelry of the Ashanti from Ghana.

Wild, primitive, dazzling or dull, but always elegant, colors are also a language, a form of expression. The techniques used for weaving, printing, and lacing are often summary and always ingenious, reinforcing still further the impression, which we in the northern hemisphere value so much, of authenticity. It is as if visual pleasure was also, already, a tactile pleasure. The trick is to melt into nature, but also to distance yourself from it by relearning its colors, patterns, and shapes, thus reinterpreting them. This is another way of differentiating nature, taming it, so that you stand out.

There is always an element of seduction in such practices and crafts. It's somewhere between playing (at being oneself) and the sacred. Only after having sacrificed at the tribal rite of passage do the young Masai Moran have the right to wear the famous purple toga. Their initiation is marked by circumcision. Formerly, their apprenticeship included a lion hunt during which the young man confronted the beast armed only with a shield and a lance. The Moran then gather in a communal hut, the *manyatta*, where their only visitors are the *endittos*, girls of the clan who are completely at their service.

Harmony of warm, brown hues: the dark woods of a table
and hand-carved bowls blend with the rusted metal
of a little garden chair (facing page).

Tapa, or bark cloth, which is found in numerous African and Indonesian
cultures, has been used as a support by artists like Miró, Yves Klein, and
Poliakoff. It is made from bast fiber, the inner bark of certain trees
which is soaked for a long time, hammered and beaten
with the aid of a mallet then decorated with stencils, combs, brushes,
rollers, etc. After drying, the colors vary from creamy white to ocher ecru
(above, work by Jérôme Abel Seguin). In the same spirit, these rugs from Iran
display subtle shades of ecru, beige, and brown (right).

This elegant dish designed by Jérôme Abel Seguin embodies all the sensuality and warmth of wood.

First the bodies of the Moran are covered in mud and their hair is braided; when the initiation is over, they can array themselves in purple—like gods, they who claim to be the "first men." The remarkable color of Masai fabrics, dazzling and dull at the same time, is probably one of the most beautiful in Africa. The dye is made with an unusual pigment found in only the most out-of-the-way places. In Africa, the pigments are the spices of fabrics. In the same way, objects in whitewood, after having been polished with the help of abrasive leaves, are given an artificial patina with vegetal or mineral dyes, fatty substances, and resins. As for masks, these are painted by means of seeds and clays. Some natural pigments were probably also imported from Asia and India, as in the case of the famous indigo dye, which was invented in the subcontinent. Indigo or ocher, red or green, there is no shortage of techniques for printing the fabrics, the *boubous*. Stencils are applied using a resin paste. Resist-printing, which is used in Sudan, the Congo, and the Ivory Coast, involves tying the fabric in certain areas at more or less regular intervals so that these parts do not become impregnated with dye.

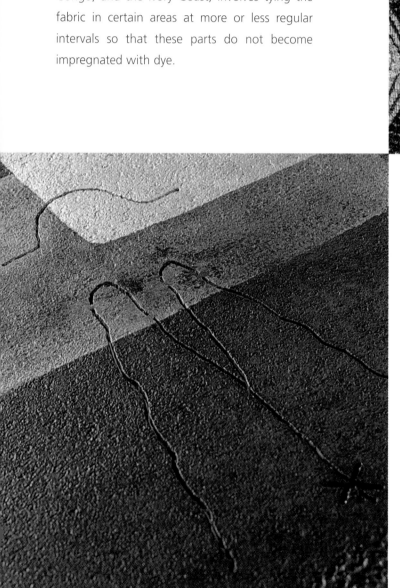

Palette of warm colors—beige, brown, earth—for this fabric with a velvety look made from raffia fibers. It was woven by women from a Kasai River tribe in central Congo. To emphasize the pattern, the embroidery is done with a needle in a lighter or darker shade (above).
Detail of a coffee table in oxidized sheet metal. The material seems to light up thanks to the nuances of its sunny colors, a combination of orange ocher, coppery red, and golden brown sienna, set off with gold (left).

We should also mention the art of *batik*, in which parts are impregnated with soap before the fabric is plunged into a bath of indigo or mud. After washing, the soaped areas are light, producing a striking effect when worn by the women. "Their maiden modesty was accentuated by the style of their clothes. They wore skirts of imposing amplitude; it took… ten yards of material to make one of them. Inside these masses of stuff their slim knees moved in insinuating and mysterious rhythm," wrote Karen Blixen in *Out of Africa*.

red and black

Red and black Igbo fabric from the Cross River region in Nigeria. The figures or animals, drawn in a naïve style, relate, as here, a tale or events from daily life (right and left). This little shopping bag in African *boubou* fabric has a woven effect (above).

A jumble of African *boubous*: indigo blue, with violet or reddish glints, originated in India, but is also widely used in Africa. Women wear blue *boubous*, generally with white patterns whose designs vary according to ethnic group and technique used—stencil, *batik*, or resist-printing (facing page, detail left, and below).

indigo

As with the earliest steps in painting and sculpture, at first it is impossible to distinguish, in fabrics or rugs, material from form, just as it is impossible to separate the body from the dancer, the trace and the imprint. But the material chosen plays an essential role. There are always five materials: a support, color pigments coated in a liquid (the binder), usually spread by means of a more fluid liquid (the thinner) on a coating, the intermediary between the support and the picture layer. This base is permanent, and has been used in the creation of pictures from Antiquity to the present day, on every continent. Strictly speaking, diluting a color means mixing the pigments of this color with an appropriate liquid.

There are a number of ancient recipes. In northern countries, eggs are often used as a base—a staple all too rare in Africa. The wealth of ingredients, for the most part, comes from both experimentation and traditions of alchemy.

polychrome

Hemp stool and oracle cup dyed in a dazzlingly beautiful orange (facing page).
Kente pagne or loincloth from Ghana, made by the Ashanti ethnic group. Draped over a window or laid on a bed,
this multicolored check design will add a bright, regal note to any room. An orange wall sets off this cheerful chair,
whose seat and back have been woven with bright blue and orange plastic cords. On the floor, the lozenge mat, also woven,
provides unpretentious decoration for a kitchen, bathroom, children's bedroom, or terrace (following pages).

The ways of treating fabrics (like the fabrics themselves) were not always invented in Africa. But they were always developed for utilitarian ends, before rapidly becoming an important manifestation of beauty and luxury. Easy to transport, the fabrics had many destinations, and also served as exchange currency. Gradually they were used along with the vegetal pagne, or loincloth, in local populations and eventually replaced it. When new techniques arrived in Africa, brought from Arabia or India (especially in East Africa), they were naturally adopted, then adapted to the surrounding colors.

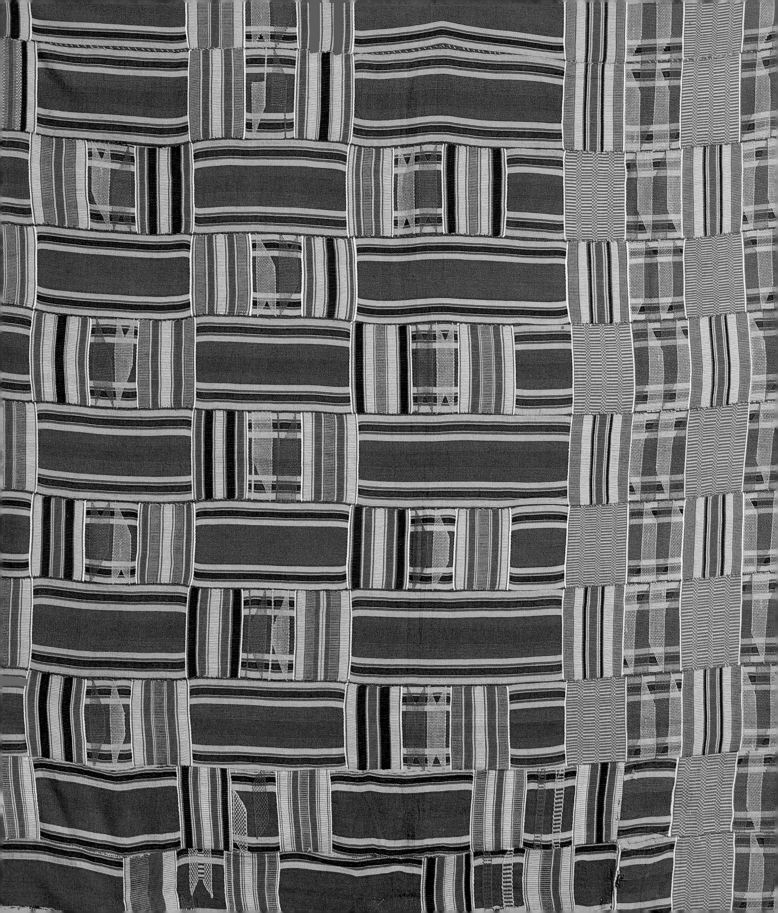

The art of recycling in the Senegalese tradition. Bursting with color, here is a jumble of multicolored heterogeneous objects—vanity case, attaché case, table, airplane—all made from tin cans, assembled according to their colors (facing page and above).

These large, strong, brightly colored bags, equally ingenious, are made out of old posters. They can serve different functions, according to their size—for example as wastepaper bins or linen baskets (right).

Panel of untreated concrete (left) or stained black (below); surprising concrete cup and candle-holder by Vincent Collin (facing page): the purity of the white and the soberness of the black answer each other in a very decorative graphic effect.

white

black

Play of cold colors for this gray, silver, black and white setting: a large settee, made up of several interchangeable felt elements, emphasizes the simplicity of the room. A simple zinc tabletop with nail decoration, placed on two monumental wooden legs, sets off the sober cylindrical lamps, made in Murano (following double page).

The black crystallizes in contact with this luminous block, while this sculpture
made of a panel of coated wood and squares of resin gives relief to a white wall (facing page and above).

For colors are everywhere, not only on fabrics. They are found on terra-cotta plates, gourds carved out of wood, fluted armchairs, and even on children's toys carved out of tin or salvaged cardboard. You should see the children, shadows on the runway splattered with sun, holding their dazzling airplanes up to the sky, improvising on a makeshift guitar (a milk packet with holes, a few fibers for strings), to appreciate the simple happiness of play, of inventing oneself.

Even more dazzling colors can be seen in the famous glass paintings by Senegalese artists. This is a revived tradition, often copied, but typical and of incredible cheerfulness. On the island of Gorée off the coast of Senegal, it is not only artists who paint: it is the duty of all the inhabitants to enhance their mud houses with patches of color. This door or that staircase is like the echo of an enormous canvas that is an invitation to dance, sing, be joyful. For this is what the colors of African style invite us and prompt us to do: to reinvent our lives, freed from the contingencies of modern life. Subdued or brilliant, they grab us by the eyes, then by the heart, with their staggering simplicity, bringing us back to the source, to the best of ourselves.

This very trendy lamp, with the look of a perfusion bottle, emphasizes the metallic glint of a chair in galvanized metal (facing page).

patterns

work by Marion Lesage

SUDDENLY, WE ENTER THE REALM OF REPRESENTATION AND THE SYMBOLIC. THE SACRED INVESTS THE UTILITARIAN. IT IS NO LONGER ONLY BECAUSE WE FIND THESE OBJECTS BEAUTIFUL THAT THEY BECOME BEAUTIFUL, THUS ACQUIRING THE STATUS OF ART OR STYLE. THIS IS MORE THAN JUST A QUESTION OF BEAUTY. IT IS THE VERY POWER OF MEANING, OF BELIEFS, WHICH CARVE THE MASKS AND WEAVE THE COSTUMES, GIVING SHAPE FROM THE INSIDE, LIKE THE BODY THAT IS SOMETIMES HOLLOWED OUT UNDER THE YOKE OF THE SOUL.

IT IS HERE THAT WE SEE HOW DIVERSE AND COMPLEX THE AFRICAN UNIVERSE IS. DIFFERENT FORMS OF EXPRESSION ARE AT WORK. THEY TAKE EVERY LIBERTY WITH THE SOLE AIM OF ATTAINING A CERTAIN MASTERY OF SUPERNATURAL FORMS. IF THEY TOUCH US SO MUCH, TO THE POINT THAT DESIGNERS, IN TURN, ARE EXPLORING THIS TERRITORY, APPROPRIATING IT FOR INSPIRATION AND IDEAS—AS IF LIBERATED FROM THE STRAITJACKET OF THEORY, "GOOD TASTE," AND TRADITION—IT IS BECAUSE THEIR EFFECT GOES BEYOND BEAUTY, BECAUSE THEY WORK ON US, BRING US BACK A LITTLE, ONCE AGAIN, TO A BEFORE, A PAST, TO FORGOTTEN SUPERSTITIONS WHICH SLEEP WITHIN US, BOTH SILENT BUT PRESENT.

WE SHOULD LET OURSELVES GO, ENCHANTED BY THE CHARMS OF THESE SUPERSTITIONS. GIVE OURSELVES UP TO THEM, AS IF WE ARE GIVING THEM THE FREEDOM TO DECORATE US—THAT IS TO SAY TO REPRESENT US. AFTER ALL IS SAID AND DONE, THAT IS THE SOLE AIM OF MYTHOLOGIES.

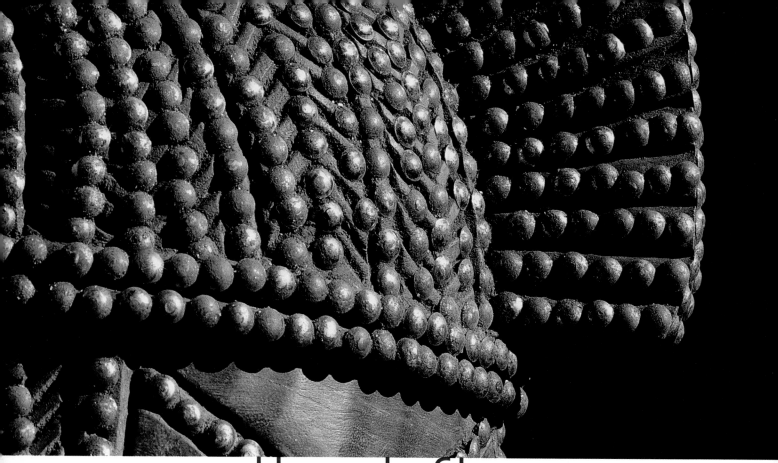

nailed finery

Again—but how could it be otherwise?—nearly all the patterns that we find on pottery, everyday objects, and fabrics were taken from nature. However, it is not simply a question of copying, of reproducing what has been seen and observed. Most people would have been happy simply to wear the skins of the animals they hunted, to make a bottle from a bladder, a loin-cloth from some foliage.

Most often, it is the vision of an artisan, his soul, which is expressed in these creations. He leaves a sign, as in the night, in order to guide his little ones, just as the female leopard holds her tail vertical: that white, almost fluorescent patch in the darkness has been there since the origin of the species.

Such signs are seen on pottery, where the decoration is made by incision, modeling, or painting. The patterns are symbolic, drawn from cosmogony, the beliefs of each tribe, each people. It is worth noting that West Africa is particularly rich in patterns of all kinds. Symbols are everywhere, and mythological representations show up on both statues and masks.

Detail of a nailed helmet with regular patterns which forms the headpiece of a statue made of limba wood from Guinea, an evocation of maternity (facing page). This sofa covered in jute and cotton is decorated with a nail motif, reminiscent of Africa (below).

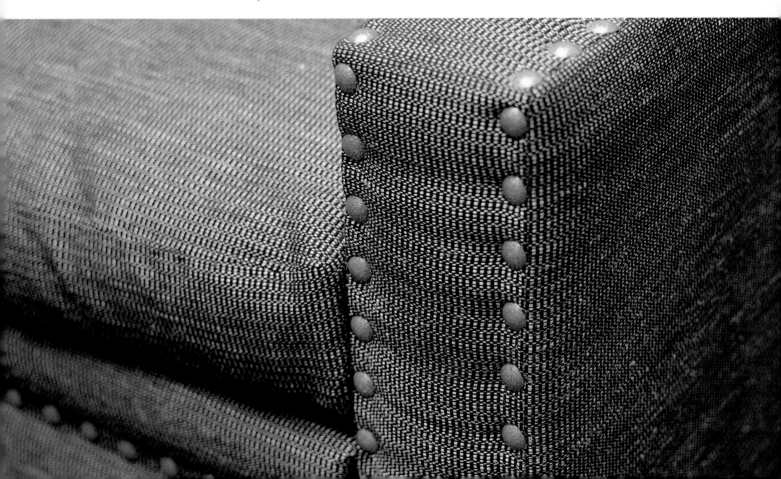

scarifications

Round shield with a central crest, characteristic of southern Ethiopia (above). Detail of the leg of a wooden stool carved all over (facing page).

Intended for funerary rites or rites of passage, masks, like the beaded apparel that often accompanies them, have the brutal beauty of a credo.

"Mysterious by nature since their immediate role… is to show ambiguous beings in action, both images and realities, the masks are closely linked to initiation," wrote Michel Leiris. Masks are the prerogative of men, of initiates. Agents of a force of which they are both the symbolic representation and the receptacle, they are worn during ritual dances, as if to bring out the essence, to express the soul. In order to conserve their "religious" character, masks should not be touched either by women or children.

Detail of a wooden door from a millet barn
in the Dogon region, in Mali. the carved figures
represent ancestors (facing page).
Mask made from black tikar wood from Cameroon.
The forehead motif, made out of copper thread,
represents a beetle, sign of happiness. This mask, whose
headdress and scarifications indicate a hierarchical rank,
is used only for initiation ceremonies (right).
The elliptical shapes of a very sculptural dish
made from burnt oak; an astonishing bowl made
from walnut, pierced by a fine laced rope,
with the look of a scar (following pages).

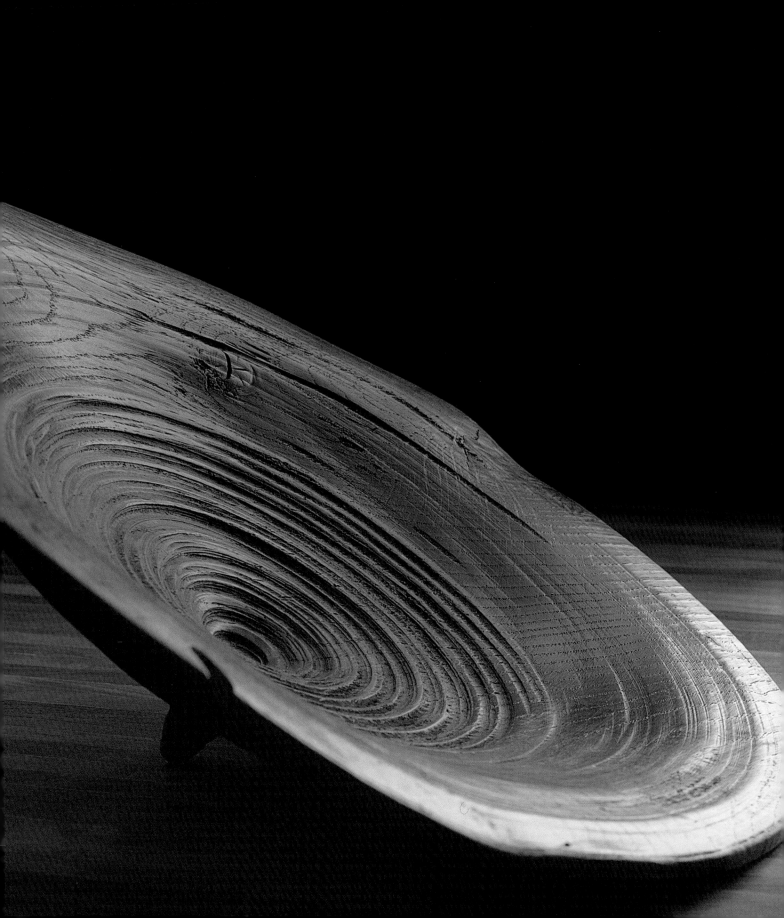

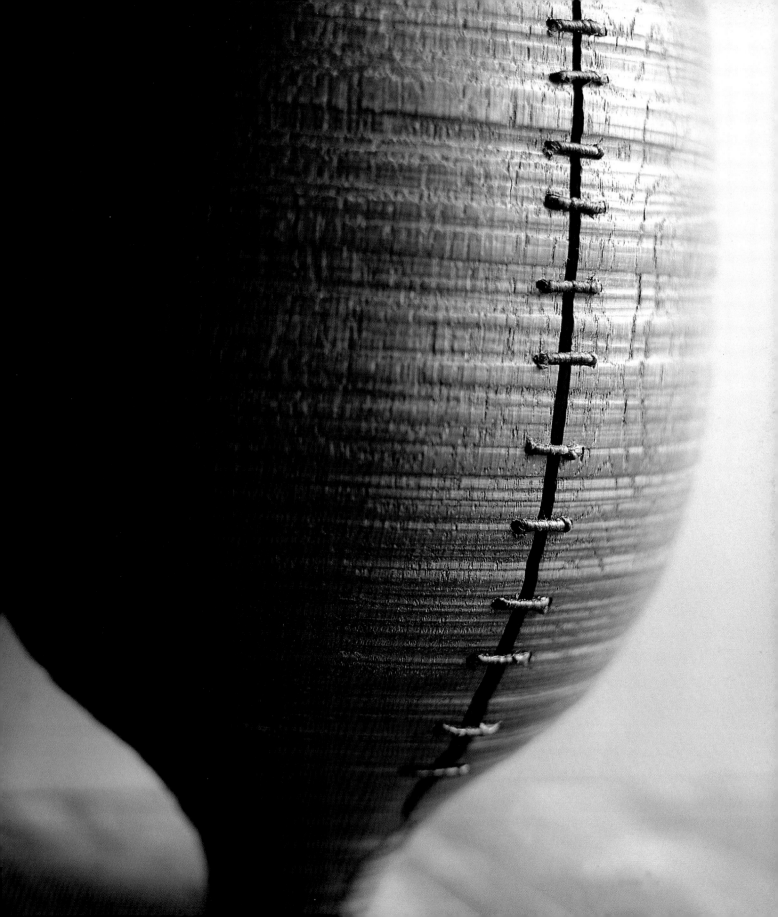

If we focus on their figurative character, the masks represent supernatural beings, between man and animal, sometimes even close to gods. And, paradoxically, it is necessary to be protected from these polymorphous beings, while at the same time trying to win their good graces.

impressions

There are all kinds of symbolic representations of masks, just as there are all kinds of patterns and sizes, corresponding to each tribal tradition.

This sofa covering is made up of strips of material woven by hand, in the village of San, in the Dogon region of Mali, then sewn together and decorated with sewn-on motifs. The designs on the cushions, on the other hand, were made by resist-printing (facing page).
Kple kple or *goli*, Baoule lunar mask from the Ivory Coast. The face is set in a perfect circle one meter in diameter. The diamond-shaped eyes are set in two ovals in the center of a regular pattern. The flat mask was used to praise peace and joy during celebrations, for example, at the time of a new harvest, or an exceptional funeral (right).
The Kuba cloths from Zaire are veritable works of art. Made using woven and sometimes dyed raffia fibers, they are decorated with appliqué motifs, and woven checkerboard designs, often placed on the edge of a pagne, as well as embroidery, which sets off geometric figures (following pages).

Thus, some of the masks made by the Kuba, who live on the plains of Zaire, are very expressive, even to the point of caricature, with their popped-out eyes, wide colorful mouths, and stringy hair, like a raffia mane. They are adorned with shells, beads, and seeds, and feature the mythical heros of the founders of the royal dynasty. The decorative art of the Kuba is also important, since all their wooden objects are carved—a demonstration of the sacred supporting art as well as the utilitarian.

For the Dogon, in Mali, where mythology always plays an essential role, sculpture has a religious stamp. It tends to neutralize the forces of life and death. The masks are made by those who will wear them for ritual celebrations, even if they are not specialists in carving. For example, at the end of a mourning period, the wearer of a certain mask will have the strength to recuperate the life force of the deceased.

The Dogon, unlike the Kuba with their naïve art, seek purity. The face of the mask is simplified to the extreme, set in a rectangle broken by a projecting nose. On the other hand, the wearer is enlivened by a costume, giving the dancer a look of ceremonial grandeur.

Kasai velvet place mats. The fabric was made in Zaire. The use of two colors emphasizes the geometric designs and the graphic quality of these textiles (left). Kuba fabric embroidered with little zigzags and decorated with cowrie motifs-white shells from the Indian Ocean which were formerly used as money (facing page).

The patterns found in Baoule art (Ivory Coast) were doubtless borrowed from their neighbors, the Senufo. But they also display a subtlety, a virtuoso use of gold inherited from their Ashanti past. Described as mannerist by some and highly prized by others for the quality and finish of the handiwork, Baoule art leaves no one indifferent. The sculptures are used for worship and have various representations: white-bearded ancestors who teach wisdom; wooden masks with wide-open mouths that exhale the divine

mixtures

Woven using a traditional technique, this print cover and unevenly striped cushions, set off by geometric motifs, are made in Senegal (facing page). "*Boubou*" shopping bag with colorful pattern enhanced by a marble-effect background (right).

breath of the Creator; half-man, half-animal creatures with supernatural powers. Baoule craftsmen bring care and preoccupation with ornament to every aspect of their daily lives. Some doors are carved with the effigies of ancestors, who guard the harvest, both literally and figuratively. Certain chiseled doors, depicting village scenes, have made their way to our antique stores and flea markets.

The designs on this vanity case come directly from the salvaged materials used to make it (facing page, bottom). A wool motif is directly embroidered on straw by Moroccan artisans (facing page, right).

Details of "*boubou*" motifs: a composition in red and yellow is structured around spirals and black triangles (above), while this stylized flower, as if seen through a kaleidoscope,unfolds in a harmonious composition of blues (right).

Another field of symbolic suggestion is the representation of woman—her femininity or fertility—a recurring motif in Africa. Whether it be to thank the gods or to implore them, it is not unusual to see masks or figurines whose faces are simply immense ovals, obviously recalling the rounded form of the mother's stomach.

In other regions, further south, among the Tonga and the Zulu, patterns and other symbolic representations (the one is not found without the other in this continent where nothing happens by chance and meaning is everywhere) are present in items made with beads, iron, leather, and feathers.

Thus it is not surprising to find these traces of primitive art first showing up in galleries, then on the walls of our living rooms, and finally making it to the fashion catwalks. Creators and designers have now arranged a telescoping of epochs, peoples, and cultures.

the play of lines

Divorcing an object or a material from its function, de-sanctifying it, is not to remove all substance from it in a spirit of playfulness, but rather to confer on it, beyond frontiers, differences, and ages, a certain permanence.

But we should reread Senghor to better understand and, above all, ensure we do not forget: "We will not leave negro-African mysticism without recalling that its symbolism is not merely an object of knowledge, but an object of practice: not only through ritual ceremonies, with their words, poems, and chants, gestures and masked dances, but above all through the life of the initiates, who live their symbolism, each in his own mind of course, and still more in his own body and soul, by transforming himself, 'converting' himself into a god, or more exactly into God."

beads

Details of of a costume in naïve style made from beads in northern Nigeria. As on certain masks, the character has scarification on the cheeks and a little cap on his head (left and facing page). Fabric plunged into an indigo bath, in which motifs appear through resist-printing; a wastebasket with an eccentric decoration made from strips of newspaper (preceding pages).

shapes

work by Marion Lesage

CLARITY AND SIMPLICITY. PURITY OF STROKE AND FIRMNESS OF LINE. POWER, BUT GENTLENESS AS WELL, AS IF MATERIALS, PATTERNS, AND COLORS HAD BEEN TAMED BY SHAPE. AND YET THEY ARE INSEPARABLE FROM IT, SINCE SHAPE HERE IS PERHAPS MERELY AN ORDERING, A PUTTING INTO PERSPECTIVE, THE END-LESS REFLECTION OF ALL THAT HAS GONE BEFORE IT. WITHOUT SHAPE, IT IS NOT CERTAIN THAT WE WOULD HAVE GRASPED ALL THE SUBTLETIES, ALL THE MEANING, ALL THE *MEANINGS* CONTAINED IN AFRICAN STYLE.

NATURE IS UNDER THE YOKE, ALL OF THE ELEMENTS ARE ASSEMBLED, THE DIVINITIES INVITED AND REPRESENTED, THE COLORS ARE IN THEIR PLACE, CULTURE CAN SPEAK.

FOR SHAPE IS THE TERRITORY OF LANGUAGE. WHETHER IT SPEAKS IN THE LINE OF A POT, THE DESIGN OF A BICYCLE, IN THE GRIEF-STRICKEN OBVIOUSNESS OF A DEATHBED, THE RUGGED UTILITY OF A STOOL, A LADLE, AN ARMCHAIR, A SIDEBOARD, OR A TABLE, IT IS ONLY EVER THE ECHO OF THE SAME ORIGIN. IT IS THE WORLD THAT BRACES ITSELF AND SPEAKS, THE REALM OF THE FAMILIAR FORGE WHERE THE ARTISAN OR ARTIST EXPRESSES HIMSELF, WHERE MAN ASSERTS HIMSELF.

ART HERE HAS SOMETHING TO SAY. TWO CONTINENTS MET ON A NARROW PATH AND THE STORY, PERHAPS, OF THIS MEETING, COULD ONLY RESULT IN AN EXPLOSION OF SHAPES, FOLLOWED BY A RETURN TO SIMPLICITY. IT IS A RECONSTITUTED LANGUAGE, STRUCTURED, GIVEN A BACKBONE THAT IS MADE MANIFEST HERE.

We can see clearly in the contemporary creations pictured here the strong influence of African art, which became all the rage in the 1920s, the roaring twenties, the heady time of champagne and Josephine Baker. We see other things, too, more serious and audacious: the groundbreaking experiments of artists.

Thus, and without getting into the kind of stormy debates that art historians enjoy, we can say that the period from 1914 to 1925, when "primitive" art was discovered by the future

totems

A sculptor and a textile designer, Malcom Martin and Gaynor Dowling, combined their talents to create these "totem" sculptures with their extraordinary shapes and suggested volumes. The wood has been carved in order to articulate and bring to life the surface (facing page). An African bowl, enameled and smoked, placed inside an embossed dish, molded on Indonesian basketwork. These objects have a fascinating form, with the rough texture of weaving, on the outside, while crackled and glossy in subtle shades on the inside (by Brigitte Banet, following double page).

Cubists, was the starting point not only for modern art, but also the still contemporary source of what we could today call African style. African art started to appear in the salons of French collectors around 1905. The Fauvists discovered African sculpture before Picasso started to take an interest in it. The latter went as far as to paint (or repaint), after this discovery, the heads of the two women in *Les Demoiselles d'Avignon*, the first painting that could truly be called Cubist.

Some people claim that we exaggerate the African influence on the art of this period, going so far as to support their thesis by quoting Apollinaire, when he speaks of African sculpture as a collection of "grotesque and crudely mystical works." Yet you need only look at certain carved Dogon doors, and the pure lines in the rows of ancestors' faces, to be convinced with your own eyes of the Cubist borrowings (see p. 86).

This bicycle made out of Indonesian wood is surely more sculpture than toy (facing page).
A traditional Lobi bench from the Ivory Coast, with its four rounded legs, decorated with a beautiful carved head (below).

primitive

It is in this light that we should see the superb and accomplished work of Christian Liaigre (see p. 139). With its purity of shape, mastery of line, and emphasis on materials, it is in itself the quintessence, the definition almost, of African style at its best and most accomplished.

So is Christian Liaigre simply, only, influenced by Africa? Is he like a designer just back from a vacation? That would be too facile. Indeed, Liaigre is above all the great perpetrator of the modernist tradition of the 1930s, the *enfant prodige* of Jean-Michel Franck, a man who demonstrated, during that epoch, that he was very much interested in African art and the "primitive" arts in general.

Christian Liaigre clearly belongs to this tradition. He works his material—the original, very African materials: wood, notably ebony, mahogany, and teak. Each piece of furniture could be described as a sort of frame, with right angles and simple, pure shapes. Liaigre excels in revealing the architecture of things. Through him, African style acquires a language and a culture that are ours.

Baoule wooden mask topped by a bird.
Highly stylized, it has two round eyes,
a horizontal mouth revealing teeth and two squat
horns meeting above a circular face (left).
These Dogon (Mali) attic ladders make it possible
to reach the doors of the millet stores. Over time, their
horizontal steps have been rubbed smooth where feet
and hands were placed. Removed from their original
function, they form beautiful decorative objects
(facing page).

The larger of these imposing wooden jars is made from black palm and the smaller from root. Originally from Indonesia, they are increasingly part of contemporary decoration. Their raw look contrasts with the low easy chair in darkened wenge, with its simple lines and leather seat (facing page). Slightly curved Ethiopian Kambatta headrest or neckrest, with carved motifs, which made it possible to protect the artful scaffolding of male and female hairdressing during sleep (above). More sober but just as decorative is this Bamoum stool, which comes from Cameroon (below).

in praise of

Slightly curved and very stretched, this traditional Lobi seat (Burkina Faso) is carved out of a tree trunk. The fact that it has only three legs indicates that it is a man's seat; women's seats have four. In spite of its imposing appearance, it can easily be carried on the shoulder. Like headrests, pipes or spoons, this object is very personal and is associated with the spirit of its owner. It is not unusual, when a dignitary dies, for his stool to be kept on the family altar as a symbol of the ancestor. Malinka (Guinea) bed for "eternal rest" used during funerals. The type of wood varies according to the size of the bed. Hence, an iroko is sometimes cut down for a dignitary, although this tree, also known as "caller of rain," is sacred (following double page).

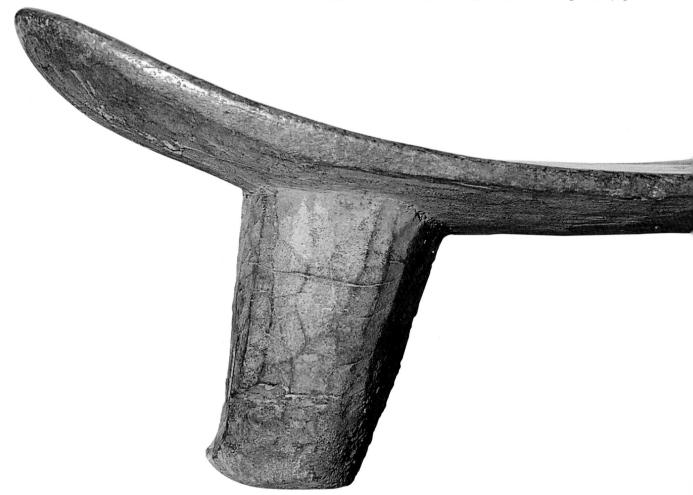

the curve

It is not a question of pillage or influence. It goes far beyond that. It's better than that, much stronger. As with the holiday villages that he also designs, inspired by lake villages in Africa, Christian Liaigre does not copy. He could adapt, but he doesn't do that either. He is simply a creator, an artist perhaps (the term is so overused), who has been able to incorporate several influences and forge them with his own vision, his own will. That could be quite a good definition of his talent, or indeed of art.

Another talent, another art: Olivier Gagnère (see p. 15). A priori, there is nothing in his work that can be directly linked to African style. Indeed, to create his objects, Olivier Gagnère uses techniques that are so difficult and so refined that they seem to distance him from this territory.

And yet Olivier Gagnère is (like Jean-Michel Franck once again) the perpetuator of the great French tradition of decorative arts—both yesterday and today. Thus, there is a clear trace of African style in the way in which Gagnère organizes and chooses colors, as well as in his use of hammered materials. His mats, rugs, and vases use geometric patterns and brilliant colors in unusual combinations. These facets of his work all link him to African style. Nor should we forget, of course, the importance of metalwork and ironwork in the decorative arts movement. But there again, like Christian Liaigre, Gagnère has made his mark.

Hollowed out of a solid piece of wood, this robust wooden spoon from Niger was used to measure out rice or manioc (above). Three bowls of great sobriety, with rounded, harmonious forms, have been placed on a tray of waxed steel, creating a very contemporary decor (facing page).

carved
from solid wood

Monumental teak armchair, whose form seems to emerge directly from the solid wood.
This exceptional work was created in Indonesia by Jérôme Abel Seguin (below).
A contorted, simple shape enhances the wood of this very raw dish by the same designer (following double page).

Instead of the artisanal, manual, crude techniques of original Art Brut, set off by a shimmering ornamentation, Olivier Gagnère substitutes very refined techniques, which he is able to make rough, natural, and original. He performs a magnificent job of structuring, and then of deconstruction. This represents a return to the source by the most difficult route possible. Culture and nature meet and mix, without it being possible for us to distinguish one from the other, to affirm the primacy of one over the other.

A playful ballet of Indonesian creepers (facing page).
An exotic usage of natural elements: horizontal and vertical round shapes combine in this coffee table and imposing room divider from Indonesia (above).

If the extreme and obvious talent of African artists resides in their ability, a priori, to visualize any shape at all, any figure whatsoever, to admit, instinctively or not, that the expression of an emotion or a belief is much more important than its representation modeled on reality—its resemblance, if you like—the contribution of Western artists and creators remains very important. Indeed, de-sanctified and offered up to the most varied of interpretations, the shapes of African style appear more alive to us, as if

pure forms

Combination of lightness and massiveness for a resolutely contemporary table with an oak base and a top in Macassar ebony (facing page). Set squarely on its massive legs, this wooden console in untreated wood emanates a natural and simple strength, as does this stool carved out of a tree trunk in which the central hole makes visible the core of the wood (following double page).

we were leaving the realm of display for the more discreet, more innocent realm of decoration, that is to say lifestyle.

We could even say that this is a kind of game, based on exchange and inspiration. African art and design interact. These are not two visual grammars clashing or trying, at the risk of losing their personalities or their roots, to crossbreed. It is something else, more subtle but also more difficult, something called freedom—the difficult freedom to be oneself.

It is a question of being able to express other feelings and sensations, the desire to bear witness to another experience, another civilization, somewhere between tradition, the respective weights of different histories, and free will.

Inspiration is no longer dictated solely by emotion but also by the traces left by respective traditions, by the imprint of cultures. Liaigre and Gagnère, as with Franck before them, serve as couriers. They transcend art and the history of their predecessors. They are like the megaphones of origins. And in these chants, they were able to mix their own voices, incorporate their own dreams, beliefs, desires… life itself.

Mammouth, a monumental sculpture made of plant material (black hemp cord) yet animal in form, sets off this tactile and sensual hemp armchair with rounded forms (Christian Astuguevielle, facing page). Pared-down lines for these "totem" candles of different sizes and wrought-iron lamp stand with glass shades (following double page).

We have come full circle. Material has been given shape. Bolstered by the various contributions and influences, the scrutiny it has been subject to, African art has become African style. Yet it has succeeded in withstanding all these assaults to retain its beauty and the strength of its origins, origins which delight and reassure us. Successful in retaining its soul, it is ready to yield to all shapes of exploitation, artistic or other. Decoration is one of the loveliest.

Thus, we welcome African art into our homes—along with a certain way of living that is (sometimes without our even knowing it) more natural, more authentic—by giving it the agreeable name of style. It would seem a good time to re-open Karen Blixen's *Out of Africa*.

"I know a song of Africa… of the giraffe, and the African new moon lying on her back, of the ploughs in the fields, and the sweaty faces of the coffee-pickers, does Africa know a song of me? Would the air over the plain quiver with a colour that I had had on, or the children invent a game in which my name was, or the full moon throw a shadow over the gravel of the drive that was like me, or would the eagles of Ngong look out for me?" Holding in our hands an object that has come from those lands, or was influenced by them, it is our turn to sing of Africa.

A lamp in the shape of a Chinese hat, goes perfectly with a modern coffee table (both by Vincent Collin, facing page).
This long coffee table by Christian Liaigre displays a very free approach to shape, with its straight lines of wrought iron and black waxed finish (below).

addresses

The following list contains the addresses of the stores, galleries, and creators who participated in the creation of this book. Most of them have several outlets in France and outside France and they will provide details of these on request.

AS'ART

3, passage du Grand-Cerf

75002 Paris

Tel. 01 44 88 90 40

Fax. 01 44 88 90 41

See pp. 3, 23 (top), 54, 55, 78-79, 84, 114, 117 (top), 118-19, 144

——

ATELIERS N'O

21, avenue Daumesnil

75012 Paris

Tel. 01 43 46 26 26

See p. 34

——

BO

8, rue Saint-Merri

75004 Paris

Tel. 01 42 72 84 64

Fax. 01 42 72 85 65

See pp. 5, 37, 96 (cup)

Also sells works by:

Catherine Grandidier for BO

See p. 75

La Mare Duchesne

See p. 18 (bottom)

Nadine Portier for BO

See pp. 104-5

Pierre Pozzi for BO

See p. 101

——

CALLIGRANE

6, rue du Pont-Louis-Philippe

75004 Paris

Tel. 01 48 04 09 00

Fax. 01 40 27 84 08

Also sells works by:

Jean-Michel Letellier

See p. 25 (top)

CARAVANE

6, rue Pavée

75004 Paris

Tel. 01 44 61 04 20

Fax. 01 44 61 04 22

Web site: http//www.caravane.fr

See pp. 38, 39, 42, 56 (bottom), 72-73, 83, 99 (right), 113

Also sells works by:

Christophe Pillet

See pp. 72-73 (lamp)

——

THE CARLIN GALLERY

93, rue de Seine

75006 Paris

Tel. 01 44 07 39 54

Fax. 01 44 07 37 51

e-mail: galleryc@aol.com

CHRISTIAN ASTUGUEVIEILLE
Bois et Forêts
42, galerie Vivienne
75002 Paris
Tel. 01 42 60 10 70
See pp. 28, 29, 65, 134, 140

———

CHRISTIAN LIAIGRE
42, rue du Bac
75007 Paris
Tel. 01 53 63 33 66
See pp. 24, 116, 131, 139
Also sells works by:
Eric Schmitt
See p. 139

———

CHRISTINE GOUMOT
trade sales
Tel. 01 45 00 11 09
See pp. 40, 41, 46, 47 (table)

———

CHRISTOPHE DELCOURT
76 bis, rue Vieille-du-Temple
75003 Paris
Tel. 01 42 78 44 97
Fax. 01 42 78 79 12
See p. 123 (table)
Also sells works by:
Brigitte Banet
See pp. 110-11 (bowls)
David David
See pp. 110-11 (place mat)
Isabelle Roux
See pp. 14 (top, left), 16, 17 (right), 19, 123 (bowls)

182 Duane Street
New York, NY

———

CONCEPT ETHNIC
5, quai de Conti
75006 Paris
Tel. 01 56 24 43 90
Fax. 01 56 24 43 92
See pp. 9, 17 (bottom, left), 66, 82, 86, 87, 91, 92, 93, 115, 117 (bottom), 120-21, 141, 143

———

CREATIONS JÉRÔME ABEL SEGUIN
36, rue Etienne-Marcel
75002 Paris
Tel. 01 42 21 37 70
The photographs were taken at Le Bon Marché,
5 rue de Babylone, 75007 Paris,
during the exhibition
"Le Monde du Bois", June 1999.
See pp. 25 (bottom) 26, 27, 56 (top), 58 (fabric, dish, console), 124, 125, 126-27, 128, 129

———

CSAO
1-3, rue Elzevir
75003 Paris
Tel. 01 44 54 55 88
Fax. 01 44 54 55 89
See pp. 20 (bottom), 23 (bottom), 31, 48-49, 59 (top), 60, 61, 62, 63, 67, 68, 69 (top), 94, 95, 97, 98, 99 (left), 100, 102, 103

———

ÉDITION LIMITÉE
7, rue Breguet
75011 Paris
Tel. 01 48 06 52 11
Fax. 01 48 06 71 58
Also sells works by:
Vincent Collin
See pp. 7, 43, 70, 71, 137, 138
Olivier Gagnère
See p. 15

———

EVANS AND WONG
Catalogue 1998-99 (on request)
Tel. 01 44 88 51 30
Fax. 01 44 88 51 32
Also sells works by:
Frédérique Morrel
See p. 32

———

HOME/AUTOUR DU MONDE
8, rue des Francs-Bourgeois
75003 Paris
Tel. 01 42 77 06 08
See pp. 57, 74, 76, 136

———

JEAN-JACQUES ARGUEYROLLES
Tel. 03 85 92 06 38
Permanent show at Galerie Vivendi,
28 place des Vosges, 75003 Paris
(Tel. 01 42 76 90 76,
Fax. 01 42 76 95 47)
See p. 59 (bottom)

———

MOSAIC
66 Green Street

New York, NY 10012
(Opens May 2000)

_____

MAISON DE VILLE

21, rue Sainte-Croix-de-la-Bretonnerie

75004 Paris

Tel. 01 48 87 80 66

Fax. 01 48 87 80 76

See pp. 10-11, 18 (top), 44.

Also sells sculptures by **Didier Pierret**

for Maison de Ville:

See pp. 22, 45

_____

MARION LESAGE

15, rue du Pré-aux-Clercs

75007 Paris

Tel. 01 45 48 32 06

See pp. 14 (top, right), 30, 85, 122;
photographed works pp. 12-13,
50-51, 80-81, 106-7, 112

_____

PM CO STYLE

5, passage du Grand-Cerf

75002 Paris

Tel. 01 55 80 71 06

Fax. 01 55 80 71 07

e-mail: pmco.style@wanadoo.fr

See pp. 33 (top), 36

Also sells works by:

Elodie Descourbes and **Laurent**

Nicolas *See p. 33 (bottom)*

_____

SAVANNAH SPIRIT

27, rue St Paul

Tel. 01 42 74 08 74

Fax. 01 42 74 08 74

See p. 90

_____

SERGE LESAGE

List of outlets on request

Tel. 03 20 48 73 44

Fax. 03 20 48 58 85

See p. 52 (carpet)

_____

STUDIQUATRE

76, rue François-Miron

75004 Paris

Tel. 01 48 87 59 27

See pp. cover, 35, 69 (bottom),
132, 133

_____

TISSAGES AÏSSA DIONE

Offices in Paris:

Maat agent

14, rue Michel-Chasles

75012 Paris

Tel. 01 43 41 27 46

Fax. 01 43 41 27 46

See pp. 52, 96

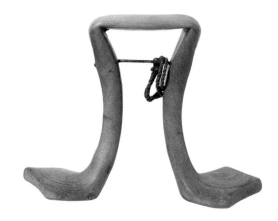

ACKNOWLEDGMENTS

Annie Desgrippes and Frédéric Morellec would like to thank Valérie Gautier, Suzanne Tise-Isoré,
Nathalie Bailleux and Caroline Chambeau at Flammarion who made this book possible,
as well as Sandrine Balihaut-Martin, Krysia Roginski and Anne Schmit.
Heartfelt thanks also go to the designers and store owners who received them
with such kindness and made it possible for them to produce this book.